CAPTURED
BY A
Whirlwind!

CAPTURED

BY A

Whirlwind!

My Encounter With The Supernatural
"WHY ME, LORD?"

Ben Soliz

Xulon Press
2301 Lucien Way #415
Maitland, FL 32751
407.339.4217
www.xulonpress.com

Unless otherwise indicated, Scripture quotations
taken from the New American Standard Bible (NASB).
Copyright © 1960, 1962, 1963, 1968, 1971, 1972,
1973, 1975, 1977, 1995 by The Lockman Foundation.
Used by permission. All rights reserved.

Printed in the United States of America.

ISBN-13: 978-1-6312-9639-0
Ebook: 978-1-6312-9640-6

Dedication

I WANT TO DEDICATE THIS BOOK TO MY Heavenly Father, whom I sometimes refer to as the Universe! He has allowed me to have this journey, with a lot of twists and unexpected circumstances, which, at the time that they happened, were mind-boggling to me. Those moments were incomprehensible, and they made me challenge His existence and ask questions about some special events as I wondered if they were merely coincidences. After all those death-defying events in my life, I realized that He was with me all the time, seeing me through when I didn't know where I was headed, loving me unconditionally despite my failures and shortcomings, and always standing by me in times of troubles. To Him, I give my endless gratitude and deep love!

I wish to dedicate this book to my little brother, Leo Soliz, who passed-away. Also, to my older brother, Edward, who passed-away at the age of two. To my father, Benito Soliz, and to my mother, Connie Soliz, who are both with the Lord.

I'd like to dedicate this book to both of my lovely daughters, Andrea Soliz and Bianca Soliz- Mcoy. I have released a mini album titled, "*Tonight with Ben Soliz*," now on most music apps, like iTunes, Amazon, Spotify, etc. One of the songs is called "Baby Eyes," and it is for both of my daughters.

I want to give a special thanks to Virginia Lawson, who herself is an author. She is the one who inspired me to write my story.

Also, I wish to give thanks to Scientist Gregg Braden, who produced YouTube videos explaining that we are all connected to the Universe and that God's signature is in our DNA. To Jake Ducey, for his videos on how we are all Divine Spiritual Beings. Finally, to Dr. Hugh Ross, for all his books on how God created the whole Universe just for us! They have been the strong force that has allowed me to remain sane despite the craziness around me. They have raised my consciousness to another level, to be in alignment with the Universe!

My warmest gratitude to Akiana Kramarick and to the movie *Heaven Is for Real,* where although she is just mentioned, she made a huge impact on me; the film also made her well known. I believe she's an angel among us! Her holy being and her story have inspired me to think and believe more strongly about the existence of God and His lovingkindness and protection over us forever!

And last but not least, to Lorelei Ralleca, for all her technical support.

Table of Contents

INTRODUCTION

The Quest for God's Existence

THERE IS AN URGENT NEED FOR ME TO write my story. A mysterious force that would not leave me alone, pushing me to reveal my story. It has taken me years to decide whether to write it or not. Is my story worthy to be revealed to the world or to just keep it to myself? I opted for the second choice. So, for many years, I kept to myself that mysterious event that has plagued me all my life with questions that will baffle me until the day I die: "Why did this happen to me, and for what purpose?" A friend of mine convinced me to tell my story because there was something mysterious and unexplainable about it, something so powerful and so miraculous, that I couldn't keep it a secret anymore. The world must know! In respect to what happened, I titled my book, *Captured by a Whirlwind: My Encounter with the Supernatural!*

So, this is my story. I will start by saying that whether you like it or not, if the Universe chooses you for a particular mission, whoever you are at that time—in my case, a poor boy with not a dime in my pocket—it is going to happen! After a magical encounter that was beyond belief, I have found God. The Ruler of the Universe accepted my challenge to appear in my life! Can you believe that? He did! And so, my story began. Possibly at that time, unknowing my unworthiness of that challenge which I voiced out, I was an immature and discontented young man at the point of despair. From then on, God transformed my life from an ordinary country boy to this person who has desired more than anything else, to be connected with His Maker.

I came from nowhere with no noble background but a humble beginning. Only my big dream to one day be in a band propelled me into the situation that allowed me to experience the Miraculous Encounter. And when it happened, nobody took notice. My friend who was with me at the time and I were in delirium about what exactly happened. And we decided to keep quiet about it, frightened about the repercussions that might come of it. We believed our bandmates might think that we were just making it up to feel important or that we were "high," and we thought they would possibly consider us weird and want us out of the band! Therefore, the decision was mutually made to keep quiet about it! But that experience, so acute and beyond comprehension, haunted me for days, months, years, and my entire life! The transformation in my life, how I now think and perceive things and relate to what matters most in life, enables others to finally see the effect of this Encounter. At best, I can say that the effect of this Encounter is my undying profession of the Existence of God!

I am so grateful and have become very passionate about many things that I had ignored before because they were beyond my comprehension. Now they become crystal clear as I have developed more strongly my awareness, deep intuition, and understanding of the working of the Universe in me!

Chapter 1

My Journey Starts

ALTHOUGH I AM A SELF-TAUGHT MUSICIAN, destiny allowed me to join several already successful bands for a national and international tour, which was an unbelievable achievement, especially for someone like me! I became the envy of other professional players who were fortunate to have a musical education and yet were not touring with professional and famous bands. As a self-taught musician who would reach that pinnacle of success, what had become of me was as mysterious as my life spent searching for the truth, which would have more impact on me for the years to come. I questioned my success and my searching for the truth, which sometimes made me feel so incomplete and created problems with my self-esteem, later making me introverted and alone, never satisfied with the glorified achievements surrounding me!

My love for music and unknowingly to me, my Lord accompanied me on this journey by trying to reveal themselves and their importance in my life! This presence of both in my life created a big conflict that played a major role in my musical performance, as well as in my personal relationships and with my bandmates.

Now, I am just happy that although I had suffered from the results of some relationships, they did not leave me indifferent but more sensitive in having them, helping me avoid the pitfalls that would put me in a depressive state, resulting in my inability to produce more and better music that I wanted. From my relationships came two beautiful daughters, whom I am so proud of because more than anything else, they deeply share with me my trust and faith in the Lord. To them, I have dedicated the first song that I have composed, "Baby Eyes," which is available on digital media.

Although, at that time, I did not acknowledge any spiritual forces in my life. All I knew was that I was playing music. But there would be certain occurrences during my journey that would make me question myself, saying, "Hey, wait a minute, I feel I've seen this place and I've been here before!" Now, as I reflect, I wonder if God was letting me know and confirming that I'm on a designated path. Or was that God's energy with the Universe, sending people or creating circumstances to put me in alignment with my destiny? I feel that my encounter with this mysterious whirlwind that entered my room was similar to events in the Bible. "Why me?" I would ask. I am nobody special. I'm not so kind or patient. I can be mean, self-centered, and rude at times.

Why have I survived this long? God has spared me from so many trials. Have I been ordained in some way to tell my story?

Chapter 2

Seeking for My Spiritual Transformation

WHY ME? THAT IS THE QUESTION THAT reverberates through my entire life. To have been empowered by a Supernatural Spirit or even to have experienced being engulfed by a mysterious whirlwind! To answer this question, I first need to take you back to how I even got to this point in my life. How did a poor country boy, a self-taught musician from Stafford, Texas, end up touring most of the United States and went on an International tour to Europe, without any formal musical training or lessons of any kind?

So, was any of this just pure luck, or was it a Divine Intervention? Should I look at this as a Supernatural occurrcncc? To move from one level in my life, a young kid, gigging music in a run-down old bar, to performing at the most prestigious hotels and resorts in Europe? Could it be that my challenge to God and the Universe was what started it all? I remember being in Cannes, France, with all the reasons to be content with my life—after all, I had a good salary, I was traveling the world, with all my expenses paid, I was gigging and meeting many talented musicians, and I had women wanting to be with me. Why was I feeling so empty? I should have been content where I was at that time in my life. I remember standing alone in the back of a luxurious hotel in Cannes, when I looked up to the Heavens and shouted out to God, "God, if You are really real, show Yourself to me!" Now, looking back, I have this realization that God has been with me all this time, but I was too blind to see. I was so busy looking for things that are not important. Still, the restlessness kept seeping in me. I suddenly felt weird too, for I was in the company of young men who were only focused on the pleasures of life. I started to distance myself and mostly kept to myself. I was afraid to tell them what I had suddenly felt, afraid they would make fun of me. I thought this new feeling might be a reason for them to remove me from the band. But the feeling of restlessness never left me.

During this journey of playing music, I would ask, "Is this real?" "Who am I?" "Has this been predestined for me?" Through the years, as I have been drawn to read more of the working of the Universe, I could not fully understand that God's energy through the Universe would send people or create circumstances to put me in alignment with my destiny. I feel that my encounter with this mysterious whirlwind that I will relate to you later in the next few chapters was a Divine Intervention—it's not something you could fathom in your deepest sense of what is normal. It was definitely an out-of-this-world experience that haunts me to this day and still seeks an explanation. It defies science, for sure!

Now, through the years, I have managed to see how foolish I have been and have drastically changed my ways. Maybe I should stop asking why and just be grateful. After all, these encounters saved me and led me on an incredible journey. For the God of the Universe to have responded to the wish of a young boy who started with just three strings on a guitar must have propelled Him to work on the mysterious entanglements that brought the right people and circumstances to make it possible for that boy's dream to come true beyond his expectations!

Chapter 3

Searching My Soul for My Love of Music

AT THE TIME, I HAD A LACK OF AWARENESS that a magical thing had been happening in my life at an early age, brought by the chain of events that seemed like only uneventful things. It had nothing to do with what I would become later in life! It was this **three-stringed guitar** that appeared in my life out of nowhere. To many who might have passed by it on a dirty country road, that

My dad's picture.

guitar looked very useless, but for my dad, who felt compelled to get this for me, the magic started. He brought it home, and for what it looked like, he too was desperate to see if something could be done with it as he handed it to me and said, "Here, son, see what you can do with it!" **As I held that guitar,** I felt my soul searching for my music to start.

My love for music had a humble beginning and quite a strange story—as strange **as that guitar was!** I came from a poor family. We were so poor that my Dad had to ride from Stafford Texas, two miles on a bicycle when he worked at the Imperial Sugar Company in Sugarland, Texas. The only luxury we could afford was when my Dad finally raised enough money to buy an old two-tone Bellaire car. There was a hole in the back floorboard through which I could see the street down below. But I thought it was a beautiful car. It was not until fourth grade that my Dad was able to give me money to eat in the school cafeteria. I had never seen so many colorful types of food before because at home, all we had was brown food—brown rice, beans, and sometimes chicken. My Dad worked sixteen-hour shifts, six days a week. I hardly ever saw him. I remember as a young kid, I would play my older sister's records and just dream of being in a band. I did not even know why

I had that desire or why I even dreamed of something like that.

Oh yes, **my magical three-stringed guitar!** How this useless, quirky instrument appeared in my life and what it did to me also became kind of bizarre. This was my very first taste of music, and it never left me alone. So, this is what happened. As my father handed me the old guitar with only a few strings on it, he said with helplessness in his voice, "Here, son, see what you can do with this." I remember going to my room and just staring at the guitar. I turned on the radio and heard a slow ballad song. I hummed the melody to myself and picked up the guitar, then on one string, I picked out the notes of the melody. I thought to myself, *Wow! This is cool.* That is when the music got into my soul!

After discovering that I could pick out a tune on one string, a lot of coincidences appeared that ushered me to where I became a member of very important bands. Were these events coincidences, or were they already planned by a higher force to allow me to work with famous musicians? I believe at that moment, a kind and loving God had seen in me a little boy who got a big dream despite his circumstances, a very ridiculous and humbling beginning but with so great desire for music and yearning to be in a band one day! He answered my heart's desire and started to shape my life to get that dream!

Let me continue to amaze you with the events that followed, after my father brought home that **three-stringed guitar.** I soon learned that a kid in our neighborhood who lived near me, Mario Carranza, had a father who could play the guitar. How unbelievable it was that the important things for me with my music were just suddenly appearing—and so easily! I will admit, though, there were some obstacles even from the beginning, such as the fact that I was terrified of this kid. He would always talk about his gangster cousins. However, I knew if I wanted to learn how to string up

a guitar, I would have to make friends with this kid, so I did. He turned out to be an alright kid, after all.

After I built up enough courage, I asked him if I could speak to his father to help me string up my guitar. At first, I was fearful to approach his father, Mr. Carranza, because

My mom's picture

he had a fearsome look about him. He was a rugged-looking man with dark tan skin because he was a yardman, always working in the sun. I was surprised when this kid Mario said, "Sure, come on, let's go to my home. I know he is home right now." His father turned out to be a very nice man too! It seemed like Somebody up there was watching me, paving my way to have a good start. The father told me to go to the drugstore and buy a set of strings. The drugstore was in downtown Stafford, Texas, about two miles away. So, I broke my piggy bank, got on my bike, and went to buy them. When I got back, Mr. Carranza strung up my guitar and tuned it. Later, at home with my newly strung up guitar, I was totally surprised that my mom got the guitar out of my hand and began to play. She knew about three chords, and she could sing! She told me she had always wanted to be a singer. She would go around the house singing all the time. Her favorite song was, "Going To Take A Sentimental Journey." Was all of this just a coincidence, or had it already been planned out for me, to later lead me to an encounter with this mysterious whirlwind, which was all brought about by my soul searching for my love of music?

While this was going on in my mind, as soon as I could play the guitar, I then learned that another kid who lived near me named Joe Salazar had a drum set and played with his father in Conjunto Band, which is a band with an accordion. Mr. Salazar played the accordion well. I began to hang out with Joe, and we played a few songs together. Hallelujah! We had a band.

To continue with my story, little events and people who had something to do with my moving on with my music just kept on appearing in my life. My grandmother lived in Rosenberg, Texas, and my Aunt Delia had a dance hall in Richmond, Texas, called Linda's Hall. My aunt let us play our little band there on Saturday afternoons.

Younger years at Linda's Hall, still unnamed band, I am the singing and holding the guitar

Later years at Linda's Hall with the band's name "The Statics." I
am on the far right, wearing a hat, playing a bass guitar.

So, while I was playing at Linda's Hall, I met a kid
named Albert Gonzales, who played bass guitar with
a band called The Silencers. They played really well.
On their break, I approached Albert and asked him
if he could show me how to play the bass. He agreed
and gave me directions to his house. Then about every
weekend, when my mom went to visit her sister, my Aunt
Delia, she would drop me off at Albert's house. Albert's
dad had an old barn where we would just rehearse and
play music. He also played the organ well, so I got on
his bass guitar and learned some songs. Then Albert
introduced me to Gilbert Flores, who was a singer and
played the guitar. So, we had it—four members suddenly forming a band—and we called ourselves The

Statics. It was such a dream, having and belonging to a band! One thing leading to another, like it was meant to happen—although, at that time, for me, it was just plain coincidences. They just happened!

Well, here is another coincidence about my turning point in my life as I began to fall in love with music! I lived in an area called Stafford Oaks, Texas, where there was a dance hall near where I lived called, Salon Morales. In later years, I would perform there with a band called The Statics.

The Statics on stage at Salon Morales, I am second from the right with the bass guitar.

The cool thing about this was that on Saturday nights, while I stood out in the front of my yard at my home, I could hear the music coming from that place. I was fourteen years old then, and that music moved right into my soul. Every Saturday night, I would walk in the dark to the salon by crossing through a tall weeded pasture to get to Highway 90, walking along the highway, passing Darnell's Gas station, then I would finally reach Salon Morales, which was always full of parked cars. I would walk to the back of the salon and peek through the old wood boards to see such great bands like Sunny and the Sunglows. They later had a nationwide hit song called "Talk to Me." They appeared on the TV show *American Bandstand* with Dick Clark. I knew then that one day, I too would be in a famous band, and my musical journey took off!

Later, while at John Foster Dulles High School, in Stafford, Texas, our band, The Statics, began to perform many times at Salon Morales when I was just seventeen years old. We even included a horn section. We played there after-football-game dances and dance-hall festivals in all the surrounding Texas towns like Sugar Land, Richmond, Rosenberg, Needville, Wharton, and so forth.

Then my life had a turning point! The Statics were playing at County Fair in Rosenberg, opening up for a very popular band called Los Muchachos (The Boys). They had a couple of albums out, and their music was being played on the radio. When we finished our set, the keyboard player of the band approached me and asked if I would hang around because he wanted to talk to me when they finished their set. "Of course," I said. "Sure!" Afterward, I met with Paul Arrendondo. He was tall and had a very close resemblance to Sean Connery. He asked me if I would be interested in joining his band as a bass player—not for "Los Muchachos," but for his band called Los Pablos.

Picture of Los Pablos Band, I am the third from the right.

They already had an album out on Teardrop Recording Label. I was very thrilled and said, "Yes!" The hardest and saddest part of this was to tell my bandmates of The Statics that I was leaving them, but it

18

was my career choice. They fully understood, and they seemed to know that I would go far with my music! So, there I was, on my next journey with my chosen band to play a different kind of music—and a better one.

While I was playing with my band, the Los Pablos, I was a senior in high school. Playing in the band while also studying was very hard for me! How I survived it is beyond me, but I got the cooperation of my teachers and their admiration, playing every weekend and sometimes during the week. All my teachers knew I was a working musician, so they let me sleep during class. Can you imagine that? Who would do that? But they did!

Los Pablos became very popular! We toured all of Texas to Arizona, Oklahoma, and Chicago! I have to say, I thought I had it made, playing with a popular band, drawing crowds, and having our songs on the radio. I never gave God any thought whatsoever. I didn't realize that He was guiding me all this time…and I wouldn't see or learn that until much later in my journey.

How did this crazy feeling for music start and eventually overtake my life? That was the question that has baffled me until this day—my love for music! For it was surrounded by many strange and completely weird things. First of all, it was somewhat pitiful. How I discovered that I love it was another quite baffling thing. I was so captivated by it that I would do anything for it, to find out how I could produce more of it, which was quite a struggle for me, but as you will see as you read further, I have continued with my journey, beating the odds and the unexpected disappointments that were in my way. Now, they simply say that I have the talent for music, that I was born into it. Whichever, I love it. I am very passionate about it and would die for it!

Chapter 4

Strange Manifestation, Is It Some Kind of a Test?

ALL I KNOW IS THAT THIS REMARKABLE thing that happened to me one strange night, out of the blue, was some kind of a test, and I am so glad that I passed it. Hooray! It is such a good feeling that somehow, I felt victorious, as it was very challenging and could easily have almost ruined my musical career. I was very young and doing very well, playing with a band. I had everything to be proud of—my youth, my talent, and my successful career playing with a famous band that had a big following. I was on top of my world, to say the least—then this wild, crazy thing happened.

When I was about twenty years old, I was running late to a gig. Los Pablos was playing at a poplar night club called the Hurricane, near downtown Houston, Texas. When I got to the night club, I could see the parking lot was full, which was typical everywhere we played. So, I double parked my car to bring out my bass case first, and I was going take it inside and let my band members know I was there. I started walking fast on the sidewalk when I saw an old man sitting on the sidewalk with his back leaning against the wall. His legs were all twisted, bent, and crooked. I still remember what he was wearing—old khaki pants, a light blue shirt, not tucked in, and brown shoes. Everybody was walking past him, paying him no attention. When I walked right by him, He looked right at me and raised his arm up, revealing his limped hand. He did not say anything, and he didn't ask for money. He just held his arm up.

I asked him, "How in the world did you get here?"

All he said was, "I live nearby. Can you help me and take me home?"

"I'm running late," I said. "Many people are waiting for me."

The old man said, "I live just a couple of streets behind the night club."

"Man, you're going to get me in big trouble," I told him. "I will be right back. Let me move my car closer to help you in." I ran to my car thinking, *Oh great, when I get back, everybody is going to be mad at me.* But for some reason, I had to help this old man—plus, nobody else was.

I pulled up in my car, double-parked again, and bent down and told the old man to put his arm around my neck. He was very light because he was very thin. I very slowly lifted him and walked him to my car, then finally got him in the passenger seat. I got in and asked him, "Ok, where do you live?"

He said, "Go around the building and turn right and go down a couple of streets." I turned on my headlights and drove. There was an old neighborhood, and about two streets down, he said to make a right turn. As soon I made the turn on a very dark street, he told me to stop.

With my foot on the brake, I looked to my left and asked, "Which house is it? It's dark out here." About that time, I heard the door open, and the old man jumped out and shut the door. I yelled out, "Hey, wait!" Immediately, I threw the gear into park and jumped out and ran to the other side of the car. Shocked that he was gone and nowhere to be found, I began to look everywhere, calling out to him. I looked in the ditch, thinking he might have fallen. I thought to myself, *How could this old man jump out of my car so fast?* I stood there by my car, stunned for a minute, and remembered, *Oh my God, I was supposed to be on stage fifteen minutes ago!*

When I got back to the club, it was jam-packed, and all the musicians were already on the stage. The leader of the band said, "Where in the hell have you been? Hurry up and plug in!" I was not myself that night because I kept thinking of that old man and what had just happened. Who could he be?

Much later in my life, I read a scripture in the Bible, Hebrews 13: 2, which says, "Do not neglect to show hospitality to strangers for by so doing, some people have entertained angels without knowing it." I wondered if that was what had happened to me, that I might have encountered an angel, and if I passed the test that God had possibly set up to see who the real me was, to see whether or not I had compassion for people who needed help. You can be the judge!

I believe if everybody looked back on their life, they would see how certain unexpected events shaped their life. Although I continued playing and touring all over, every once in a while, I would remember that old man, whom I had helped, as he kind of taught me to continue having compassion for people.

Chapter 5

My Musical Career on the Rise with a Lot of Unexpected Turns

OF COURSE, NOTHING EVER STAYS THE same, and this was so with my music career! My life was about to take another drastic turn. Our band's album was hitting really well in Arizona, so we were constantly going to Phoenix and other cities in that state…when the crap hit the fan. Our sax player—I will only use his first name, Jerry—confronted Paul, our bandleader. Jerry said that he had spoken to the promoters who were booking us and found out how much Paul was get-ting paid, which was in the thousands. Paul was paying us very little, which was only peanuts compared to the amount he was getting from the promoters. He was pocketing most of the money. But honestly, that did not bother me. Paul provided the vehicles with all the upkeeps, and he paid for the gas, hotels, and suits we wore. Plus, I was young and having the time of my life. That did not matter to me because Paul was doing all the bookings, providing his own vehicles for transportation, and it was because he had all the connections to get us to perform. Everything had exploded, and it all came to an end. Just like that! I never had any animosity towards Paul.

Now, after what happened in Phoenix, Arizona, I was being pushed in a new direction. Was this just a coincidence, or was there a Higher Power directing my life? The guitar player, Pete, and I decided to regroup as a four-piece band. I called my buddy Albert Gonzales, whom I had played with years back when I was in The Statics. He was a keyboard player, the guy who helped me learn the bass guitar. I asked him if he would be interested in joining us. He said, "Sure," then we recruited the drummer, Sergio, and we were off and running again! It was really easy to get Teardrop Recording Label to back us up. The label changed their name to Latin Soul.

So, we began writing and recording some music under the name Joshua. Not long afterward, a big recording artist from Mexico recorded one of our songs, "Avioncito de Papel," which put us on the fast track. Was I just lucky, or was I being guided? We began getting good royalties and receiving huge gifts from our Latin Soul Recording Label. We started getting a lot of attention, especially Pete, because he sang most of the songs. However, all the popularity pushed him into the spotlight, and he lost it. He could not handle it. He lost his mind, and his actions became so foolish and weird that we could no longer work with him. What is crazy is that he did not drink alcohol or do drugs. Again, I hold no grudges against Pete because I know now God had other plans for me.

So here I am, again being pushed in a new direction. I did not know what to do, and I began asking, "What in the world is going on?" I did not consider God or even think of Him. I soon became very depressed and got irritated about any little thing that came to me. I was so uptight that I did not care to associate with anybody. I needed income, so I got in a local three-piece rock band in Houston. We called ourselves Mexicali Rose, but I needed more money, so I got a job at a printing company, A-Jiffy Printing. It was alright delivering prints. Our guitar player also needed a job, so I got him a job where I worked. His name was Artie Villasenor. Other musicians soon needed jobs, so I got a job for another musician named Robert Ceballos, a drummer. The thing about Robert is, he worked with an amazing keyboard player name Lanny Peach, a professor at The University of Houston. Lanny had this incredible way about him that amazed me. I asked Robert what it was about Lanny, why he always seemed so calm and cool. Robert said that Lanny had been studying the art of Transcendental Meditation (TM). I asked Lanny about TM, and he told me that if I was interested, I should go to this address he gave me. TM changed my life! It helped me get rid of major stresses in my body. I was able to connect with the world and the Universe, and it gave me a sense of energy and strength. Was knowing about TM a coincidence, or once again, was this an intervention for me to find myself, to discover who I am?

Getting back to the rock band…they cared nothing about writing music. They just wanted to play at the local bars, which made me very disappointed. I just aimlessly just existed. That's when luck stepped in again. One time, I was at a bar, just having a drink called Loneliness, when a girl approached me and asked for a cigarette. Her name was Carolyn. She found out I was a musician and told me of a great band called Apocalypse. I thought, *What a weird name for a band,* since "Apocalypse" means destruction or disaster. I never liked the name, but this band was amazing; they had cool harmonies and the musicians were top-notch. I was playing on the weekends in downtown Houston at the Phase III Night Club, and she asked me to meet her there. Carolyn introduced me to the bandleader Jack Martinez. Jack sang with The Commands. They had a hit song titled, "No Time for You," and Jack was also a former member of the band called, the Royal Jesters, plus a few members of the group Apocalypse were former members of the Royal Jesters, too. Their famous song on the charts was, "That Girl," a great song with horns and great harmonies. When I told Jack that I was a bass player and vocalist, he told me that they were needing to replace their bass player and asked me if I was interested. I said, "Sure!" I gave Jack my contact number, and bam! I was off again!

At this point, I was saying to myself, "Wow! Am I that lucky, or is Somebody up there helping me?" I never thanked God for all of this because at that time, I was so absorbed with my music and myself that I was not realizing the role of God in my life, despite so many events that were telling me this Great Being was working on my behalf! I was very foolish and blind not to have seen God and the Universe working on my behalf.

Let me go back to my music and my band, Apocalypse, which I joined.

Picture of the band, "Apocalypse." I am on the far left.

Soon, we became the house band at the Golden Fleece night club at the market square in downtown Houston, playing five nights a week. The club could seat four hundred people, and we would pack the place, standing room only, which was up to a thousand people.

After being with the house band for three years, it started to become a dread. Many times, I was not in the mood to play music, sing, or even go out to the night club, but this was the life I had chosen, or the life that was presented to me. To get in the mood, I began to drink, but not heavily until later. Plus, people sending drinks up to the stage did not help. The people enjoyed the musicians getting plastered.

Now, the band was getting bored and tired, so we decided to move to another city. We moved to San Antonio, where all the musicians were from. Immediately, we got a house band gig at a popular San Antonio night club called Heaven. We packed the place, and all was well…until I began drinking more heavily. Right before we stepped on stage, I would take a shot of Everclear, a 151-proof liquor, and a shot of tequila. We were the house band for about a year, and we began to play at other night clubs in and around San Antonio. Everywhere we played, we usually had a crowd show up.

Then my life began to take a drastic turn once again, sending me in a different direction. Now, I believe I was being led toward my spiritual encounter! We were to play at a very nice night club called The Grand Hotel. The place was full; all of us were backstage, when, right before we were to go on stage, the lead singer, whom I will just call Ambrose, approached me and said, "Ben, I want you to know that nobody comes here to see you!"

I replied, "Hey man, let's just be thankful they are coming and not think about if they are coming to see anybody in particular." It never crossed my mind that they were coming to see me.

He responded, "Well, just know they're not coming to see you!"

"Ok, whatever, man."

Dang! What a way to set the mood. Now, I had to go perform like everything was beautiful. I was so deeply disturbed by his words that I could not wait for the set to be over. Finally, when the set ended, I went straight to the bar to get my usual strong alcoholic drink, a shot of Everclear and tequila. Ambrose came to the bar, and this man approached him. I was close enough to hear what that man said to Ambrose. He said he was from Dallas, Texas, and had a booking agency called The Directors Agency; he needed a band to back up his singer and tour. Ambrose told him that he was not interested and walked off. Well, the Universe came to my aid again. I introduced myself and told him I would get a band together and back his singer. He said, "Ok, let's talk," and gave me a business a card. I just want to say I hold no grudges against Ambrose and I have forgiven him, because this event lead me to tour with a better band.

The next day, I met the owner of The Director's Agency. He told me the singer's name was Wayne Shannon and that he was the drummer for Gary Puckett and the Union Gap. They had many big hits like "Woman, Woman" and "Young Girl." What the public does not know was that when Gary got sick, Wayne took over singing and was the voice on some of the songs. That did not matter much to me; all I knew was that I had to put a band together quickly. "Okay," I said. "What is the name of Wayne's band?"

He said, "Universe."

I thought to myself, *Hmm, that is interesting,* and told him I liked that name, "Universe." I told the other guys in Apocalypse and asked the guitar player and the keyboard player to join me.

Now, all I needed was a drummer. That night, I went to the Navy Club, a late-hour bar, and spoke to Jackie, the drummer. He was sold and signed on. So, it was time to begin rehearsing the setlist I was given for Wayne Shannon because I had to be in Hitchcock, Texas, which

This is the actual newspaper clipping of our band "Universe" scheduled to perform on February 18th somewhere during the 1980s.

was a three-hour drive, in two weeks to perform.

I had to rent a large trailer and haul all the band's equipment in my car. The back bumper got severely damaged and almost fell off. I was so thankful they had a large school bus that was modified with a loading ramp to carry all our band equipment. We even toured all over Texas, Louisiana, Tennessee, Missouri, and Oklahoma.

I soon moved to Dallas, Texas, which became my home base, but then it hit me again! Wayne started in on me. The band would play a dance set before the show, and the drummer and I were the singers. Then Wayne would come on; he sat up in the middle of the dance floor and would do his thing. I thought he was very good. Then the band would finish the night with our set. Well, Wayne began to do some weird things. He would jump on stage during our dance set and just act like an idiot. We started having arguments about nothing. I just wanted to play, but Wayne felt I was drawing too much attention away from him. Musicians are sensitive and very insecure.

Yep! You are right—another change in my life. Well, I went back to Dallas and enrolled in school to learn studio recording; suddenly, out of nowhere, I got a call from San Antonio. It was Henry Lee, a well-known keyboard player who played with Sunny and the Sunliners. I did not know him very well, and I had no idea how he got my number. He came straight out and said he was the musical director for The Platters, and he needed a bass player; he asked if I was available to perform in two weeks in Dallas. I told him, "Yes!" He called just at the right time. He then told me to get ahold of The Platters' *Greatest Hits* album and learn all the songs—they had sixteen number-one hits back in the '50s.

Henry Lee, asked me to meet him at this high-profile dinner club in two weeks. I was so excited, so I did like he asked and showed up in my old tuxedo; the night went perfectly. We did a great show and received a standing ovation. After the show, Henry said they were about to go on a five-month tour and asked if I wanted to join them. I said, "Count me in!" He told me to go to the airport the following week, where there would be a paid airline ticket to Indianapolis waiting for me. He would pick me up there with my equipment.

What astonished me was how the Universe—I don't want to confuse you, I'm talking about the actual Universe, not the musical band—knew I was going to be home in Dallas, to get that call from Henry Lee, because he had called me on my landline in my apartment. Very strange, indeed!

The next thing I knew, I was in the air flying to Indianapolis. By the way, I do not like flying. When I got there, a twelve-passenger Winnebago, with a dining table, eight bunk beds, and a restroom, was waiting for me. Wow! Hey, I'm just a poor country boy from the cotton fields of Stafford, Texas, about to embark on an incredible adventure! After playing all around the northern states—Michigan, Pennsylvania, New York— we headed to Las Vegas, Nevada. Yes, we drove. Playing Las Vegas, Reno, and Lake Tahoe was so cool! I couldn't help asking again, "Is this all just luck, or am I being directed by some Higher Power?"

Picture of "The Platters," I am on the bottom row, second from the left.

Chapter 6

Challenging God and His Existence

I NEVER KNEW EXACTLY WHAT THIS TURN of events would lead to. At this point in my career, life was going too fast for me to even comprehend it. It was like being on a roller coaster! I didn't have time to think. The impact of my rising career had a kind of domino effect. I had no control, no grip on anything, with one thing leading to another.

After spending a few months in Nevada, the band and I headed to San Francisco, California. Next, we were dropped off at the airport. I didn't really question anything because I didn't care; just knowing they would put me on stage was all I cared about. This time, I asked

Henry Lee, what was happening. "Why are we here at the airport, and where are we going?"

He said, "We're going to Europe to start a tour."

"Huh?" I was more concerned about the flight there. I asked how long the flight was.

"Oh about sixteen hours," he replied.

"Oh, really? Wow!"

As we boarded, I couldn't help but feel how amazing it was for me to be at this point in my career, and especially in my life. Again, I have to bore you with a reminder of my humble beginning: a poor country boy, who barely made it through high school, with no musical training, with no bank account and no money saved, was walking onto an airplane headed for Europe. How could this be?

After the long flight, I just stared out the airplane window, looking over the ocean. When we finally landed in London, we had to catch another flight to Cannes, France. We stayed at the most luxurious resort right on the Mediterranean Sea. We performed there, and everybody loved us. Then we went to Holland to perform, then back again to Cannes.

A picture of the "Platters" at the Resort & Hotel on the
Mediterranean. I am at the far right.

We stayed there for about three months, playing in
and around France and Holland. I was living a dream,
right? So, I wondered, *What in the world is wrong with
me?* I asked myself, "Why do I feel so empty and not
happy?" I was gigging. "I have an excellent salary; I
have women wanting to be with me. Isn't that what life
is all about? Ok, how about those people who are not in
music? What is life all about for them? To have a good
job, come home, watch TV, go to a sporting event on
the weekends, or for some, to go to church on Sundays.
Is that all there is to life?"

I went to the back of the resort, where I knew I
could be alone, and I looked up to the Heavens and

spoke to God out loud. "GOD, if You are real, reveal Yourself to me!" Did *You* put that Sun up there? Did *You* put the moon and stars up in the sky at night?" This was my challenge to God! After that, I felt much better because I had made my petition. I left it up for Him to show Himself to me.

Chapter 7

Mysterious Encounter

OUR EUROPEAN TOUR WAS OVER, AND WE headed back to the states. I must say, I couldn't wait to get back to Texas to eat a real taco and have some refried beans. But first, we had to go to Louisville, Kentucky, where The Platters were scheduled to perform at a hotel night club there. When we got there, I learned the sheriff of that city ran the night club and he was the one who had brought us there.

We stayed and performed there two nights. On Saturday night, before the gig, I went to the hotel bar to have a drink and sat at a table to listen to the music, when I noticed a beautiful girl sitting one table away from me. We kept glancing at each other, so I asked her to dance. She got up and walked me to the dance floor.

While dancing, the Sheriff walked up to me and showed me his gun! The Sheriff asked, "How would you like a bullet in your gut? This is my woman!"

I said, "Ok, she's yours! Here, take her!" I then walked backstage and did our last set.

As I was getting ready to go to my room, Miss Benedict, the manager of The Platters, told me that the Sheriff invited all of The Platters and the band to his house for dinner the following evening. I thought, *Oh, great! I get to have dinner with the man who earlier threatened to kill me.*

Sunday afternoon, at about 4:00 p.m., I was just relaxing on my bed, reading a magazine. I was rooming with the drummer, whose name was Ray, and he was also relaxing on his bed, reading. Our room was on the second floor, facing an open field. The door was a heavy metal door that would automatically lock when closed. My bed was closest to the door.

All was quiet and calm, when suddenly, the door burst open, hitting the wall with a loud thud. To my astonishment, a whirlwind of some kind positioned itself at the doorway. It just whirled there for a few seconds. The crazy thing is that it gave off a low humming sound. Nothing like a rushing sound of the wind. It did not engulf the whole room with the wind, but this

Whirlwind then began to slowly move into the room right in front of my bed.

No wind of any kind was even touching me. As it moved across the room along the wall, it passed the vanity mirror, where all our music charts were stacked. Suddenly, our charts started flying up in the air. Ray and I just watched the Whirlwind, then, in a trembling voice, he said, "What is that?" I did not answer because I was in disbelief about what I was seeing, and I felt no fear. The Whirlwind moved to where our tuxedos and shirts were hanging. We could see the arms of our coats fly all around.

Meanwhile, Ray and I were completely untouched by this thing that entered our room; I did not even feel a tiny bit of wind touching me. Then it moved toward Ray and surrounded him. I will never forget the look on his face; it was a look of sheer terror, and his hair was flying all over the place. Then his hair settled down, and I thought to myself, *I'm next.*

The Whirlwind surrounded every part of me, from my head down to my toes. I could feel my hair flying franticly all over the place. There was this very gentle feeling, just like the feeling of a cool breeze, like when walking by a stream or near an open meadow. I felt peace move down deep into my blood, soul, and spirit.

It felt like I was using Transcendental Meditation, but much deeper.

Then I felt my hair settle, and the Whirlwind moved to the doorway and just remained there for a few seconds, until it grabbed and shut the door with a loud bang! In a quivering voice, Ray again said, "What was that?"

I answered Ray in a slow, sleepy voice, "I don't know." It did not make any sense at all to me. Why did this Whirlwind appear suddenly in a quiet room? It was a very spectacular moment, and I was beyond belief! This could not be happening! What drove it and who sent it to be in the room where I was?

When the Whirlwind was surrounding me, I had a wonderful feeling, and I heard a soft voice coming from it, saying, "Do not be afraid. Everything will be alright!" When the Whirlwind left, Ray shouted again in a loud voice, "What was that?"

I told him, "Relax, it's okay," and I fell into a deep sleep and Ray did too!

Chapter 8

A Death-Defying Threat: The Sheriff and His Doberman Dog

THE EPISODE OF MY LIFE I AM ABOUT TO share with you is an incredible, surreal, and out-of-this world experience—a death-defying incident that could happen only in movies. But it happened…and to me! Every time I think about it, I often even ask myself, "How did that happen? Who am I to be spared from such a terrible, dog attack?"

As I woke up that morning after the "Whirlwind event," I was still in awe; I couldn't think or speak about it. I would try to say something, yet nothing came out of my mouth. It was an incident that you could not talk

45

about just in plain language. To Ray, the Whirlwind event was kind of a nightmare, and as we looked at one another for an answer, we knew any answer would be elusive. So we left it at that, to be quiet about it. Between us, we acted like it never happened. Although this supernatural event occurred, at that time, I did not know what it meant or why it happened. But now, as I looked back, I can see that it was God's intervention in my life, guiding and fighting me.

Later that evening, I was in this spiritual mood when the hotel phone rang; it was Mrs. Benedict, the manager for The Platters. Ray answered the phone and told me that our tour bus would be there in forty-five minutes and we should get ready. I swear, when I put my feet on the floor, I could not feel the floor. It was like I was floating. Ray and I did not say a word to each other. It was like we were in a trance or a dream. When I walked to the bus, I felt like I was flying because I could not feel my feet.

I got on the bus and we drove for about an hour, way out to the countryside where the Sheriff lived. When we arrived, I saw a big house with a huge front yard with large trees. I was not feeling any fear, and I didn't have any thoughts of his threats. When I walked into the house, the first thing I noticed was this large, long living room. At one end of the room, I saw a large green cushiony seat, so I made myself comfortable on it.

A short while later, in walked the Sheriff, with a black-and-brown Doberman dog, who had a harness around its neck, which he held by the handle. The dog was calm. I was calm too, even though I am terrified of dogs because of what happened to me when I was about eight years old. A German Shepherd attacked me and knocked me down to the ground. I can still remember the dog having his legs on either side of my head, growling one inch from my face, about to bite my face off, until its owner ran out and saved me.

The Sheriff was at the other end of the living room. When he saw me, he pointed to me and gave a command to the dog: *"Kill!"* Instantly, the dog turned into this raging, evil, mad demon beast, just barking very loudly and revealing his large teeth to me. Meanwhile, I was just sitting still on the seat, in a state of complete calmness from my encounter of being captured by a whirlwind earlier that day. The Sheriff was struggling to hold the dog back.

Miraculously, as he was bending down, trying to pull the pin on the handle, in an instant, I heard a voice, the same voice that had spoken to me when the Whirlwind came into my room: "Get ready, look to your side, grab his son, put him between your legs, and put your arms around him." As the Sheriff finally released the pin, the dog came charging at me. Suddenly, I was staring at death right in the face. I never even noticed this little five-year-old boy. Who could this boy be? When the dog was within inches of me, I did what the voice had told me to do. The Sheriff gave the dog another command: "Heel." The dog sat on his stomach and laid his head at my feet. I will never forget the look on the Sheriff's face. His mouth drooped down, and a completely dumbfounded look appeared. When I saw the Sheriff's face, I broke out laughing very loudly and uncontrollably at the whole situation, which rather strange, especially looking at the dog. I remember I had tears in my eyes.

I could not stop laughing. If you have ever witnessed a Holy Spirit laughter, well, it was just like that. With his head hung low, the sheriff walked up, grabbed the dog, and left the room. Moments later, his wife walked up to me and told me that was the most incredible thing she had ever witnessed. She said that the sheriff did this stunt to terrify and humiliate people he doesn't like, and he would let the dog chase the victim outside the house, all over the yard. I hardly remember the rest of the evening, and the sheriff said nothing else that night.

The next day, I got up and went to have breakfast because I knew the tour bus was going to pick us up to take us to our next gig. When the bus got there, I walked back to the bar to have one last look around, when I saw the Sheriff playing cards with a group of people. I do not know why, but I walked up right next to where he was sitting and just stood there for a minute. The Sheriff hung his head down and would not look up at me; he didn't say a word to me, and I didn't say a word to him. In my way, I was daring him to say that his evil ways would never succeed, as there is a God higher than him Who oversees everything. I just felt justified by not showing him any anger and just let karma deal with him! Still having that heavenly feeling after the Whirlwind encounter, and being saved from that death-defying threat, I just hope that the sheriff finds peace in his life! For I have forgiven him.

I then walked off, never to play in that city again, but the memory of that incident never leaves me and brings me this realization of my Maker, my God, Who was so protective over me to make such a spectacular and unbelievable display of shielding me from such a heinous act of murder. Again, I ask, "Why me, Lord?"

Chapter 9:

The Revelation of Truths

I BELIEVE WHAT ENTERED MY ROOM THAT day penetrated me deep down in my soul and changed me forever. What is so incredible, is that this Force seemed to know the future, and it came to strengthen me. But why? Was it because while I was in Cannes, France, I had made my request to God to show Himself to me? Well, I believe He did, in many ways!

I continued touring with The Platters, but my heart was not in it. I could have stayed with them. The organization even approached me and said they liked my singing and playing and asked if I would consider doing something on my own. They would back me up—a real amazing opportunity, but I passed it up.

So, I gave my notice and moved back to Dallas, Texas, still searching for answers. When I returned to Dallas, I was just roaming around, not really in any direction. I became depressed. I thought, *What in the world is wrong with me?* To make ends meet, I got a gig at a local bar in Dallas called The Filling Station. This rich kid named Danny kept coming to the bar and introduced himself to me. We were talking, when he asked what I did during the day. I said nothing and told him that I could use a day gig. He asked if I would like to be his chauffeur and just drive him around. Wow!

Hey dude, you got yourself a driver. Danny owned a 300-unit apartment complex, and I took him to his meetings, but he mostly wanted to party. I was not too happy about that, but he also gave me a free apartment to stay in. What in the world was the Universe up to? Well, when there was nowhere to drive Danny, he would ask me to walk around the complex and just see how the tenants were doing. One day, I found an old small, beat-up New Testament Bible in a vacant apartment that Danny owned, which he had asked me to go check out. I picked it up and said to myself, "Ok, God, I heard that all the answers are in this book. I'm going to read this and see." So, I just started to read it like any normal book. The New Testament starts with the Gospel of Matthew. It was tough reading because it goes through pages of this genealogy. I thought, *What a waste*, but I made a promise to myself: I was going to read that little handheld book to see if there were any answers that I had been searching for: Who put the sun, moon, and the stars up in the sky? Why can see in color? Why is this heart of mine pumping nonstop, and who started it? Later, I found out that if you translate those names in the genealogy from Hebrew into the English language, they are sentences.

After reading the Bible for a few weeks, I was saying to myself, "What? There is this Man who has all this power of the Universe, who no man has ever seen, and He is saying He is here to serve us? Huh? No way a man could have written this. Give any man on this earth any type of power, and they will want to rule and force you to bow to him. But not this Man! He says to wash each other's feet and help and love one another. If you look at the history of humankind, we always are at war. If I had any power, I would punish everybody that has ever wronged me. But man, Jesus says to forgive those who have wronged me."

One night, as I was reading the Bible, there was a knock on the door. I thought, *Huh? I live at the very back of the apartment complex. Who is going to walk back here and knock on my door?* I decided I was not going to answer it and they would go away, but they kept knocking, so I got up and went to the door. When I opened it, there were two young men standing there, and one said, "Do you know Jesus?"

I was kind of perplexed. I told them, "I just started reading this book to find some answers, and here you are at my door."

One of the two men at my door said, "Later on this evening, not far from here, we are having a gathering to talk about Jesus, and we would like for you to join us."

I said, "Sure! I want to learn more about Jesus." They gave me directions.

When I got there, I did not know anybody, so I looked everywhere for those two men that came to my apartment door, but they were nowhere to be found. *They probably have something else to do,* I thought. So, I sat alone. Then I started to look around. I noticed on the altar was a large container full of water. There was this preacher who began to say that one needs to be baptized to be accepted and enter the Kingdom of God, then the Holy Spirit would help one to find the truth. I got myself baptized because I wanted this help and needed answers.

After the service that evening, I knew and felt that my life had changed and that I would be going to a *new and different kind of incredible journey!* The next day, I went to Danny's office, ready to be a chauffeur, for which I was a go-to a person. They asked what had happened to me. I said, "I found Jesus!" I started to profess that Jesus is the Son of God! They laughed and asked if I was going to be a Jesus Freak now. Huh? Is it being a freak to want to believe that all is well and to learn how He paid your penalty, being crucified on the cross? I learned later in the words of Jesus in Matthew 10:32-33 32 Whosoever therefore shall confess me before men, him will I confess also before my Father which is in Heaven. 33 But whosoever shall deny me before men, him will I also deny before my Father which is in Heaven.

Now, once again, I felt it was time for me to move on. I could clearly see that I did not fit there, working for Danny, so I packed up my things and moved back to Stafford, Texas. I thought it was time to give up this crazy notion about living my life as a musician and get myself a decent job, stay out of trouble, get old, and die. It is kind of funny because every job I had ever gotten during my life, I would only last about a year or two. I would either quit or get fired, not realizing God was not finished with me.

Conclusion

I AM CONTINUING WITH MY INCREDIBLE journey, but this time, God is on this journey with me! During my searching for answers and truths, I learned that God has always been in my life, but I was blind to see Him. Everything that happened to me during my adventures, whether good or bad, was the that GOD was guiding me. The first of GOD'S intervention was when my father brought home that old three-stringed guitar. That started the whole ball rolling, and that was when my dreams began. One thing after another, GOD was taking me higher and higher, only to take me to the point where I asked myself, "What is life all about?" Finally, I asked GOD to show Himself to me.

If you take the time to reflect back on your life, you will see how a certain event caused you to turn to another direction. I don't have any kind of holier-than-thou attitude, for I am learning that Christ actually makes me feel just the opposite; I have concluded that

I'm no better than a poor beggar, a homeless person living on the street, an alcoholic, or someone doing time in prison.

I try to be a better person and have higher aspirations for a higher self and mind! I have learned to research and listen to people with great minds, like scientists with their profound knowledge of the Universe and the truths that they have discovered with the existence of God. I am so excited to know that GOD will never abandon us humans, as He has implanted His imprints in our DNA. The whole Universe has been created for our planet Earth, and there are higher dimensions in which we are meant to live. I have learned so many other great things that I can't put them all in this book, but I want to invite you to do the same—to continue with your search for the truths and hidden mysteries of the Universe that are waiting to be unfolded! Be empowered by the real truths and knowledge that are out there! I owed this knowledge to Mr. Gregg Braden, an American author and scientist, geophysicist, linking science and spirituality. Mr. Jake Ducey, an author of The Purpose Principles and Profit from Happiness, and Dr..Hugh Ross an Astrophysicist and a spiritual speaker.

And for my Bible study, I have learned so many marvelous things of God's love, His great Providence! It has made me aware of the love, the sacrifice, and the death of His Son on the cross to save us! The life and stories in the Bible have suddenly become alive for me; they are not just events that happened thousands of years ago! In the Bible, you can find the truths about your own life now! As I said, I am still on my journey of awakening! I have awakened into so many truths. At this point in my life, I have my spiritual awakenings!

As for my music, it is and will always be a part of me. It has always been intertwined with my spiritual journey and awakening. I have not abandoned it; my music is totally under God's control and gives me great joy. So, now and then, I join my former bandmates for a gig here and there. And you would be surprised to find out that most of my friends have given up their music. At this age, I have renewed a deeper interest in composing music. Music is in my soul! That is the one thing that started this journey anyways, and even this book! I have been able to produce an album titled *Tonight with Ben Soliz*. I did everything in the album—I played all the instruments, did all the vocals, and composed all the songs. I am very proud of the hard work that I put into it. Now, I am Live, and you can download my music from iTunes, Amazon, Spotify, Deezer, YouTube Music, Google Play Music, and other digital media music apps.

I have learned from Gregg Braden, that appreciation, gratitude, compassion, and care can harmonize your heart and brain. I feel that by enveloping yourself with great desires of what you wish for and surrounding yourself with the answer that you are looking for, you will be in alignment with the Universe. I have experienced extraordinary events that have baffled me about my existence, which somehow, I needed for my complete transformation from an uncaring unbeliever to this person who is seeking out to connect to this Wondrous Great Power and to know Him more!

Along my journey, there were people who might have hurt me intentionally or unintentionally, and I might have responded unkindly to them or thought of them negatively. To these people, I would like to say that I totally forgive them, and I would like to borrow a Cherokee Indian saying, "Chante Ishte," which translate to: "The eye of the heart, which does not judge!"

So long! I hope you have the time to listen to my music, and I wish you good luck on your own personal journey!

I base my whole life's existence and future on these verses, my favorite scriptures:

> **Romans 8:1-2: Therefore, there is no condemnation for those who are in Christ Jesus. For in Christ Jesus the law of the Spirit of Life**

has set you free from the law of sin and death.

About the Author:

BEN SOLIZ HAS BEEN A BIG DREAMER! Despite his humble beginning and with just a 3-stringed guitar, he dreamed of joining a famous band at a very young age! Nothing stood in his way for his great love for music. It was almost a total salvation for him to have it, to search his soul for his love of music. Such a great desire for music got into a spiritual quest so that his music got intertwined with the search for his soul! The combination of both catapulted him into kind of stardom, his dream came true playing with a famous band like "The Platters" as their bass guitarist. It was hard to imagine that such a thing could happen to a young boy whom he said traveled around the world with a famous band with no dollar in his pocket to start with. As a writer, his spirituality and love for music have been reflected in his writings. He is very passionate to unravel his soul and his quest for a higher identity. He knew that other than this physical make-up and force that he needs to deal with every day, that there is a Higher Being who watches him, protecting him and loving him as evidence of how he had escaped life-threatening situations! His reluctance to why such incredible happenings did happen to him came to the incessant question:" "Why ME, Lord?" He wrote simply but powerfully. You can't help being there yourself, feeling the fear, the ecstasy of the moment, especially when he wrote about his Miraculous Encounter with God and the unbelievable and bizarre circumstances that followed it! His writing is very moving, so vivid and poignant and engaging but elevating and inspirational, giving hope to people who feel themselves alone with their struggles!

Composed and Produced by the Author.

CPSIA information can be obtained
at www.ICGtesting.com
Printed in the USA
LVHW022305280720
661581LV00009B/641